the girl's guide to loving yourself

November, 2006

Palynn,
You are an amazing young lady
and are capable of moving the
world with your own two hands.
Remember how strong you are and
that you're destined to do great
things. I am so proud of
who you are!
Remember to love yourself!

Love,
Carrie

TO KATIE K. FOR BEING JUST AS CRAZY AS I AM.
TO KATIE S. FOR TRYING YOUR BEST TO KEEP US SANE.

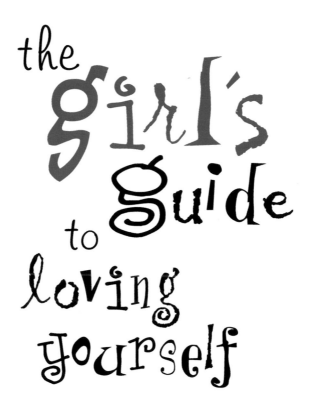

the girl's guide to loving yourself

a book about
falling in love
with the one person
who matters most...
you

diane mastromarino

Blue Mountain Press™

Boulder, Colorado

We wish to thank Free Spirit Publishing, Inc., for "A person with an eating disorder might..." from TAKING CHARGE OF MY MIND & BODY by Gladys Folkers, M. A., and Jeanne Engelmann. Copyright © 1997 by Gladys Folkers and Jeanne Engelmann. All rights reserved.

Library of Congress Catalog Card Number: 2003011644
ISBN: 0-88396-751-0

Certain trademarks are used under license.

Manufactured in the United States of America.
Second Printing: 2004

 This book is printed on recycled paper.

Library of Congress Cataloging-in-Publication Data is available.

Blue Mountain Arts, Inc.

P.O. Box 4549, Boulder, Colorado 80306

CONTENTS

what it's all about...

Loving yourself isn't about looking in the mirror and feeling satisfied on the one day that your jeans fit just perfectly and your new haircut looks great. It's not about wearing the clothes everyone else is wearing even though they make you feel uncomfortable on the inside. Loving yourself isn't about depriving your body of the nutrition it needs because you need to fit into some trendy outfit. It's not about dropping your real friends and pretending to be someone you're not in order to hang out with the "in crowd." It's not about running on the treadmill for four hours a day or drinking 14 gallons of bottled water after skipping breakfast.

Loving yourself isn't about following the dreams your parents created for you because you're too scared to hurt their feelings or too lazy to dream up your own. It's not about making decisions based on what everyone else is doing or not doing. In fact, loving yourself has nothing to do with anyone else at all. It just has to do with you.

Loving yourself means you have the highest respect for your mind, body, and soul. It means you know who you are and who you want to be. It means you have great dreams and want to do everything in your power to ensure their realization. When you love yourself, you care enough about the person you are to say no to things that could possibly harm you or have a negative effect on your life. It means you think about the outcomes and don't just act on impulse.

Loving yourself means you want to be as knowledgeable as possible about your body and the way it works, and you aren't embarrassed to ask questions you wish you knew the answers to. It means you try your best to create positive relationships with your friends and family. Loving yourself means you have the courage to be unique and to be "you," not some carbon copy of the latest fashion model on the cover of a magazine. It means you won't change yourself to fit the needs of your current, ex- or hope-to-be-soon boyfriend. Loving yourself means knowing how great you are and not letting any person, any place, or any thing ever get in the way of that.

GET REAL. Get real **FRIENDS** who like you for who you are and who aren't just talking to you because of the **CLOTHES** you're wearing or the guy you're **DATING**. Get a real **STYLE**, one that **DEFINES** who you are; don't just **STEAL** someone else's to **FIT IN** or **LOOK COOL**. **GET REAL** about your **DREAMS**; they are yours to **CREATE** and yours to follow.

Get real **ACTIVITIES** and **HOBBIES** that you **WANT** to be doing… ones that make you **HAPPY**. Get real about your **BODY**; be the **BEST YOU** that you can be instead of trying to fit some **RIDICULOUS IDEAL**. Get real about **LIFE**; it's yours. **NEVER FORGET THAT**.

get comfy

One thing you should strive for in your life is comfort. I'm not talking flannel sheets and pink fuzzy slippers comfortable. I'm talking getting comfortable with who you are, where you are going, the goals you set, and the path you choose to reach them. Being comfortable means that you feel good about yourself and about the kind of person you choose to be.

If you walk around with butterflies in your stomach or feel uneasy from head to toe (or anywhere in between, for that matter), you are far from being comfortable. You need to figure out what is making you feel this way and change it. Comfort comes from being yourself. When you are completely real, you feel confident knowing you are a strong, free-willed, powerful girl who makes her own decisions and chooses what path she will take. You don't have any reason to pretend you're someone you're not because you are completely comfortable being you.

LESSONS LEARNED THE HARD WAY: 1) THE COLOR OF THE GIRL'S HAIR ON THE BOX OF HAIR DYE DOES NOT IN ANY WAY REFLECT THE COLOR YOUR HAIR WILL TURN IF YOU USE IT. 2) JUST BECAUSE EVERYONE ELSE IS A REDHEAD DOESN'T NECESSARILY MEAN YOU SHOULD BECOME A REDHEAD. 3) A BASEBALL CAP CAN REALLY BE AN EXCELLENT FASHION ACCESSORY.

being you is always in style

Being you isn't a fad that comes and goes. It doesn't have to cost your entire allowance or be an exact replica of what everyone else seems to be wearing. Being you stays in style because it defines who you are. There's no reason for you to feel pressured to look a certain way. I know, I know… easier said than done. The truth is, when it comes to fashion, certain styles look better on some girls than they do on others. The clothes you choose to wear should reflect the kind of person you are; they should make you feel good about yourself and your body.

You have your own body type and your own sense of style. Put those two things together and you can create a super cool wardrobe designed especially for you, by you. There's nothing better than that. When you are 100% yourself, you have no reason to feel anything but great. You can walk down the street feeling proud and confident. You are cool and comfortable and looking your very best. Now if that's not style, then I don't know what is.

LESSONS LEARNED THE HARD WAY: 1) WEARING A HALF-TOP IS NOT VERY SEXY WHEN YOU CROSS YOUR ARMS OVER YOUR STOMACH BECAUSE YOU FEEL EMBARRASSED ABOUT HOW YOU LOOK. 2) SOMETIMES, WHEN YOUR MOTHER SHARES HER FASHION OPINION, SHE ACTUALLY DOES KNOW WHAT SHE IS TALKING ABOUT. 3) HALF-TOPS ARE HIGHLY OVERRATED ARTICLES OF CLOTHING.

love me (for me) or love me not

So you've got a certain boy on the brain, and of course you want him to notice you. The question is, how do you get that to happen? You can run around wearing skimpy clothes, hoping he will notice you that way... but chances are he will think you are a different type of girl than the kind you really are — and then you may find yourself in over your head. You can drop your friends to hang out with the crowd he usually hangs out with, but you will end up losing real friends and faking who you are to try to fit in with your new ones. You can follow him around and worship the ground he walks on, but he will probably end up walking all over you. Even if any of these actions land you a little bit of attention from this certain someone, it definitely won't be the kind of attention that lasts.

The best way to get his attention is not to beg for it. Just keep doing the things you always do. The more fun you seem to be having and the more you seem not to care, the more likely the chance he will begin to care. There is no need to profess your love to him, but do make an effort to let him know you're around. Make small talk or conveniently forget your watch and ask him for the time. Be totally yourself, and if he likes you, that's cool. If he doesn't, it's his loss. With this approach, you just may score your dream guy, and you will keep true to yourself in the process.

LESSONS LEARNED THE HARD WAY: 1) IF HE TALKS TO YOU ON THE DAY YOU WEAR YOUR SKIMPIEST OUTFIT AND NOT ON THE DAY YOU WEAR A BAGGY T-SHIRT AND JEANS, HE'S NOT WORTH YOUR TIME. 2) IF YOU DROP YOUR FRIENDS TO JOIN THE CROWD THAT HE HANGS OUT WITH, CHANCES ARE THAT IN THE END, YOU MAY JUST END UP ALONE.

real friendship

Real friends like you for who you are. They respect your opinions and believe in your dreams. They don't judge you by your appearance, or popularity, or by the guy you are dating. They know all the little details about you and still like you anyway. Real friends are there to celebrate the happy days and to console you through the not-so-happy days. Real friends laugh with you and cry with you and feel for you when you don't feel much like feeling.

Not everyone who comes and goes in your life will prove to be a real friend. Some people may seem that way for a bit, but when the going gets tough, those people are usually hard to find. It's been said that once you grow older, if you can count the number of real friends you have on more than one hand, you are a very lucky person. Trust me when I say that this is very true.

Value your real friends. Don't waste time with people who don't respect you or who really don't listen when you talk. If you can't be completely yourself in front of someone, then that person is not a real friend. Put 100% into friendships that matter and don't be fooled by people who give you any less.

LESSONS LEARNED THE HARD WAY: 1) WHEN NEW PEOPLE START PAYING YOU SPECIAL ATTENTION AFTER YOU GET A BRAND-NEW CAR, THEY ARE NOT REAL FRIENDS. 2) WHEN YOU LOCK YOUR KEYS IN THAT CAR AT 3 A.M. IN THE POURING RAIN, 30 MINUTES OUTSIDE OF TOWN, THE PERSON WHO PICKS YOU UP AND LAUGHS WITH YOU ABOUT IT THE WHOLE WAY HOME... NOW, THAT'S A REAL FRIEND.

the bully blues

In every school there is at least one bully. Someone who thinks they are more powerful than most. Someone who puts other people down to make themselves feel bigger. Bullies exist not because they are bigger or stronger or cooler or better, but because they make people think they are all of these things. In reality, bullies are just regular kids looking for attention and a way to feel important.

The truth is the only reason bullies exist is because other kids allow them to. Most kids fear standing up to a bully so they take a step back and allow the bully to make them a victim. Other kids join the bully so they can avoid getting picked on. Deciding how to handle the situation is not easy. The one thing you know for sure is that hurting someone else's feelings is wrong and getting your feelings hurt doesn't feel good at all. No one has the right to belittle another person or make them feel scared, or sad, or uncomfortable inside. When faced with a bully, keep that in mind and never ever forget it.

LESSONS LEARNED THE HARD WAY: 1) IF YOU BEFRIEND THE BULLY AND BEAT UP ON OTHER KIDS, YOU MAY NOT GET BEAT UP YOURSELF. 2) THE GUILT AND HURT YOU WILL FEEL INSIDE WILL BEAT YOU UP A LOT MORE THAN THE BULLY EVER COULD.

dealing with bullies

- **Have confidence.** Even if you don't feel like it, be confident and act brave. Work on your posture. Stand tall and walk proud. Keep your head up high and act as if nothing in the world can bring you down. If you believe this is true, other people, including the bully, may believe it, too.

- **Ignore the bully.** Act as if you could care less about the bully's words or actions. Don't run away as if you are scared, but walk away as if you have better things to do. (You probably do.)

- **Be loud and say no!** Sometimes the bully won't let you just walk away. If there are people around, say no in a loud, strong voice. Don't insult the bully, but rather tell him or her that what they are doing is wrong. A loud shout can end a fight before it even starts.

- **Check in with yourself.** Take a HUGE deep breath. Tell yourself you are okay and replace any harsh words you heard from the bully with kind words from yourself. Repeat things like: "I am strong," "I am confident," "I am beautiful."

- **Be a buddy.** If another person is being bullied, tell the bully to stop. Others may join in and the bully may give up. Make a pact with friends to stick together and help one another feel confident, instead of scared.

- **Seek help from a teacher or parent.** Teachers and parents can be a great help in stopping bullies. You may be concerned that if you tell, the bully will be angry with you and things will get worse. Voice your concern to the teacher or parent, and together you can work on a way to deal with the situation.

ACTIVE-ities

Do you think Madonna refused to join the choir because some kids thought it was geeky? Or that Mia Hamm, the soccer queen, didn't play soccer because no one else was playing it? Probably not. Yes, it's true many activities do come with stereotypes. *It's uncool to do this; only the brainiacs are part of that.* But the truth is all types of kids do all types of activities. Activities are what you make of them, and if you make them fun you'll find that they create wonderful friendships, build lots of self-esteem, and even relieve tension and stress.

Choosing what activity you want to join shouldn't be based on what other kids are doing or not doing. It should be based on your own likes and interests. If you don't know exactly what those are, then just try a bunch of things to learn what you are good at and, more importantly, what makes you happy. So dance, run, learn, experiment, create, sing, act, jump, sew, swing, and cheer your way to finding a better, more active, and involved you!

LESSONS LEARNED THE HARD WAY: 1) THE PEOPLE WHO GET LOTS OF PICTURES IN THE YEARBOOK ARE THE ONES WHO ARE OUT THERE DOING LOTS OF THINGS. 2) WHEN YOU FLIP THROUGH YOUR YEARBOOK AND THE ONLY PICTURE OF YOU IS YOUR CLASS PHOTO, YOU'LL WISH YOU'D GOTTEN MORE INVOLVED.

follow *your* dreams

A lot of times it's hard to hear your own thoughts over your parents' nagging, your teachers' advising, your counselors' counseling, your friends' gossiping, and all the other zillion people who feel that you will be better off hearing their opinions. It's so easy to get caught up in what other people think is best for you, and it's even easier to lose yourself in other people's dreams.

So what is it that *you* want? Your answer is probably some variation of "How the heck am I supposed to know?" In your heart, maybe you do know. Maybe you think your dream is so far-fetched that it could never happen for you. Maybe it's something that is unusual or uncool, so you are embarrassed to pursue it. Maybe it's something completely the opposite of what your parents hoped for you and you're afraid of hurting their feelings. Or maybe you have no clue what you want. Regardless of your answer, regardless of what your dream is or what it will be someday, do yourself a favor and make sure that whatever it is, it is yours. Dream *your* dreams, and when they come true, you will be so glad you did.

LESSONS LEARNED THE HARD WAY: 1) IF YOU FOLLOW SOMEONE ELSE'S PATH, CHANCES ARE YOU WILL TURN AROUND SOMEDAY AND HAVE TO START ALL OVER AGAIN. 2) NOTHING IS IMPOSSIBLE. 3) DREAM BIG.

a little thing called... confidence

confidence

Be **CONFIDENT**. It sounds so **SIMPLE**. But to be able to walk into a room and feel completely **COMFORTABLE** with who you are, with **HOW** you look, with **WHAT** you know, with **WHOM** you know… now that is **ANYTHING** but **SIMPLE**.

Having **CONFIDENCE** means that you feel good about yourself both **INSIDE AND OUT**. It means that you are comfortable in your **OWN SKIN**. It means that when you **WAKE UP** in the morning and look in the **MIRROR**, you are **HAPPY** with the person you see (despite the **BED-HEAD** and **MORNING BREATH**, of course). And at night, when you lie down to **GO TO SLEEP**, you really feel **GOOD** inside.

confident vs. conceited

So let me guess... you're worried that if you have some confidence and feel good about yourself, people may think you are conceited. The truth is, there is a huge difference between being confident and being conceited. Having confidence in yourself is recognizing your worth and taking pride in who you are and in the things that you do. This is not to be confused with walking around with your nose in the air, bragging about how perfect you are, and expecting other people to worship the ground you walk on. (That would be being conceited.)

Confidence isn't about proving to others how great you are; it's more about how you feel inside about yourself. Just because you have confidence doesn't mean everything will always run smoothly. A confident person may get butterflies in her stomach when speaking in front of a group of people. She may fumble over her words or get sweaty palms when the boy she has a crush on asks her a question. But a confident person knows that she has the capability to chase those butterflies away and compose herself the best way she can. She knows that she can do anything she sets her mind to, and she believes in herself. Once you can do that, you can do anything.

LESSONS LEARNED THE HARD WAY: 1) IF YOU BELIEVE INSIDE THAT YOU ARE A COOL PERSON, OTHER PEOPLE WILL BELIEVE IT, TOO. 2) IF YOU CONSTANTLY TELL PEOPLE HOW INCREDIBLY COOL YOU ARE, NOT ONLY WILL THEY NOT BELIEVE YOU, BUT THEY WILL LOOK FOR REASONS TO PROVE YOU WRONG.

saying "thank you"

How many times has someone paid you a compliment only for you to find some ridiculous reason not to accept it? If you are like most girls, you shrug off compliments, saying that you owe your beauty to some new pair of jeans or to a new haircut. Or your face gets flushed, your cheeks get all rosy, and you find yourself in the midst of that oh-so-unpleasant and uncomfortable silence. You should take a compliment for what it is… something special that someone took the time to notice about you.

The next time someone pays you a compliment, say "thank you" with pride and tuck it away for the days when your ego needs a little extra boost. Don't reply to compliments with negative responses, shrugging them off as no big deal. They are a big deal. They are the little extra bits of positive energy you need to love yourself that much more.

LESSONS LEARNED THE HARD WAY: 1) IF YOU CONTINUALLY GIVE SOMETHING ELSE THE CREDIT FOR THE COMPLIMENTS YOU RECEIVE, PEOPLE WILL HESITATE TO GIVE THEM TO YOU IN THE FUTURE. 2) YOU WILL MISS THOSE COMPLIMENTS IMMENSELY ONCE THEY'RE GONE.

your worst enemy

Feeling confident is by no means an easy thing to do. Sure, you can blame your parents and teachers and anyone else who puts too much pressure on you and has super high expectations. You can say that it's their fault you feel a little less than confident these days. But chances are there is someone else in your life who should really be taking a lot of the blame… and that person is you.

You can be your own worst enemy most of the time without even realizing it. You expect so much from yourself physically, mentally, and emotionally. You look in the mirror and tear yourself apart because you look or act a certain way. You compare yourself to other people and constantly tell yourself that you fall short. How would anyone be able to feel confident with all that criticism?

Instead of comparing yourself to the people around you, take the time to figure out the things that you like about yourself. Every time you wake up in the morning, think of one thing that makes you feel happy about being you, and remember that thing throughout your day. Don't let anyone discourage you, and definitely don't discourage yourself. Having confidence really feels good. Don't just take my word for it. Try it for yourself.

LESSONS LEARNED THE HARD WAY: 1) TELLING YOURSELF YOU'RE BAD AT SOMETHING WON'T MAKE YOU ANY BETTER AT IT. 2) TELLING YOURSELF YOU'RE FAT WON'T MAKE YOU ANY SKINNIER. 3) TELLING YOURSELF YOU DID A GOOD JOB AND THAT YOU ARE PROUD OF YOURSELF WILL, WITHOUT A DOUBT, MAKE YOU FEEL GOOD INSIDE.

praise yourself

Every day, whether you realize it or not, you do something that deserves praise. The world may not stand up and take notice all the time, but that's not its job; it's yours. Don't wait around for people to recognize what you do. They are busy doing their own things and searching for other people's recognition. You want to set yourself apart from them.

Having confidence means you are not on a constant search for other people's approval. Of course it is nice to be praised for what you accomplish, but you can't be dependent on that praise. Other people may not recognize it, but you do so much throughout your day that makes a difference in the world, and these are things that you should take pride in.

At the end of the day, you should be able to name at least one thing you are proud of having achieved. Regardless of its size, you make a difference in the world each and every day, and if that's not a reason to be filled with confidence, then what is?

LESSONS LEARNED THE HARD WAY: 1) SCORING A FREE TUBE OF LIPSTICK THAT THE CHECKER FORGOT TO RING UP DOES NOT WARRANT PRAISE. 2) TAKING IT BACK AND PAYING FOR IT DOES.

whiz-dom

Let me be the first to tell you that smart is anything but dorky. Smart is in style; it's the reason why cute oval glasses are trendy and why bookstore coffee shops are always crowded.

Being smart is a huge part of being confident. I'm not saying go lock yourself in your room and read the encyclopedia until you're blue in the face. But just think about how much better you'd feel about yourself if you could walk in on any (okay, almost any) conversation and share a little insight.

It's easy to stick to what you know, but where's the fun in that? Put yourself in environments that will expand your knowledge. Pick up a book you wouldn't normally read. Talk to someone who has a completely different background or heritage from you. Ask questions. Don't be embarrassed that you don't know the answers. Learn as much as you can. You will be happy that you did.

LESSONS LEARNED THE HARD WAY: 1) NEWT GINGRICH IS A WORLD-RENOWNED PUBLIC SPEAKER AND A FORMER MEMBER OF CONGRESS, NOT A CITY, STATE, OR TROPICAL ISLAND. 2) THE WORD "NEW" CAN EASILY BE MISTAKEN FOR THE NAME "NEWT," AND IF THAT HAPPENS TO OCCUR, IT CAN MAKE FOR AN INCREDIBLY EMBARRASSING MOMENT.

tell it like it is (even if it's not)

Most of us have tons of knowledge stored away in our pretty little heads, but when it comes to using it, we take a step back. Be confident in what you know and in sharing it with others. Don't fret: you won't be pinned as a geek for knowing what's going on in the world or even for knowing what went on years and years before you were born.

Sometimes when you're not sure of yourself, you may decide that it's better to keep quiet rather than to say something and be wrong. You may be afraid that if you are wrong the people around you will laugh at you. But chances are that many of those people are thinking the exact same thing, and if you speak up, all of you will leave the experience learning something new.

Confidence isn't about always being right. It's about feeling good enough about yourself to share your thoughts and ideas with the people around you.

LESSONS LEARNED THE HARD WAY: 1) WHEN YOU THINK YOU KNOW THE ANSWER IN CLASS, TAKE A CHANCE. RAISE YOUR HAND AND SHARE IT. 2) IF YOU DON'T, YOU WILL SPEND THE ENTIRE REST OF THE CLASS, MAYBE EVEN THE REST OF THE DAY, KICKING YOURSELF UPON HEARING YOUR CLASSMATE STATE THE ANSWER YOU KNEW IN YOUR HEAD WAS RIGHT.

Lately your **EMOTIONS** are all **OUT OF WHACK**. Yesterday you **CRIED** because someone looked at you funny and today you **FEEL** like all you want to do is **LIE IN BED** and **LOCK YOUR DOOR** to the world. Things are more **CONFUSING** than they used to be. Some days you want to **CURL UP** in your mother's lap and have her tell you a **BEDTIME STORY**. Other days you want to do what you want, **WHEN YOU WANT**, and have **NO ONE** tell you otherwise. And then just when you're **THINKING** you're totally **OFF THE WALL**, you start feeling **PRETTY GOOD** again.

Should you look into getting one of those special **WHITE JACKETS** and check yourself into a **MENTAL** institution **ASAP?** No. This emotional **ROLLER COASTER** is completely **NORMAL**. Your **JOB** is to learn to **DEAL WITH IT**.

emotional roller coaster

You're growing up, and your body is doing a complete 360° (without your permission, of course) and going through changes you may or may not be happy about. With all of this going on, it's no surprise that you're on an emotional roller coaster these days. Your moods are swinging all over the place and there are many times you probably feel overwhelmed and out of control. Don't fret... Sad but true, this is completely normal.

You probably find yourself getting totally upset over something that may not even have bothered you a few months before. Perhaps tears well up in your eyes for no reason at all or the things that used to make you happy don't anymore. You are undergoing lots of transformations, some that you can see happening and some that you can't. It's scary to grow up and feel everything change and to know that you have no choice but to change along with it. It makes complete sense why you are feeling the way you do, but don't tuck everything inside you. Don't let your emotions get the best of you. Though sometimes it may seem otherwise, remember that you are in charge of how you're feeling, not the other way around.

LESSONS LEARNED THE HARD WAY: 1) WHEN YOU DON'T DEAL WITH YOUR EMOTIONS, THEY WILL BUILD UP AND MOST LIKELY ERUPT AT EXTREMELY INAPPROPRIATE TIMES. 2) IF THE INAPPROPRIATE TIME HAPPENS TO BE YOUR BOYFRIEND'S GREAT-AUNT'S FUNERAL, YOU WILL WISH YOU HAD DEALT WITH YOUR FEELINGS EARLIER.

me, myself, and i

The one person in your life who knows you the very best, who will always stick by you, and who will never leave you is "you." You are the only person who knows when you're having a rough time and when your confidence meter is falling below average. Only you know exactly what you need to hear to get yourself back on track and feeling like the superwoman you really are.

The power your mind can have over you, both emotionally and physically, is incredible. No matter what you encounter, whether it is as little as taking a test in school or as big as giving a presentation in front of a crowded auditorium, if you can convince yourself that you are okay, you will be okay. Taking control of your emotions is the best way to work through them. If you have to leave a room and chat with yourself, go right ahead. Do whatever it takes to give yourself the pat on the back you need to get you through the moment. You have what it takes to do just about anything, and anytime you feel a little less sure about that, turn to the person who knows you best for a little support... you.

LESSONS LEARNED THE HARD WAY: 1) TAKING DEEP BREATHS HELPS CALM YOU DOWN SO YOU CAN THINK RATIONALLY AND GET CONTROL OVER YOUR EMOTIONS. 2) TAKING DEEP BREATHS ALSO PREVENTS PASSING OUT WHILE SINGING AN 'AMERICA THE BEAUTIFUL' SOLO AT THE FINAL BASKETBALL GAME OF THE SEASON IN FRONT OF PARENTS, FRIENDS, AND THE CHEERLEADING SQUAD.

the fear factor

Everyone gets scared at one time or another. That's the truth no matter how big you are or how tough you can be. Some people are afraid of things like being in the dark or flying in an airplane. Others are afraid of things like public speaking or being called on to answer a question in class. Fear is a very normal and healthy emotion.

When you are scared, your body may feel funny inside. You may breathe faster, your hands may get sweaty, and butterflies may start fluttering inside your tummy. You may even feel a little dizzy or get a stomachache. These things happen because your body is getting ready to deal with whatever situation is causing you to be scared. Your blood pumps quicker through your heart and rushes to your hands and feet, preparing them to move quickly, and your lungs breathe faster to supply your body with more oxygen.

Fear is normal, but it shouldn't happen all the time or get in the way of doing the everyday things you like to do. If you feel scared a lot of the time, you should talk to a parent or teacher about it. They may take you to a special doctor who can help you learn how to relax or prescribe some other treatment to help you work through your fears.

LESSONS LEARNED THE HARD WAY: 1) BEING AFRAID OF THE SOUND OF THUNDER, OF A ROLLER COASTER, OR OF MAKING A SPEECH IN FRONT OF A HUNDRED PEOPLE IS COMPLETELY NORMAL. 2) BEING AFRAID TO GET OUT OF BED, TO WALK ACROSS THE STREET, OR TO BE AROUND OTHER PEOPLE IS NOT SO NORMAL. 3) IF YOU ARE AFRAID ALL THE TIME, SPEAK TO SOMEONE ABOUT IT. 4) GETTING HELP WILL CALM YOUR FEARS AND HELP YOU TO FEEL YOUR BEST.

get out

You're not going to feel 100% all the time. No one does. There will be days when you are feeling kind of down on yourself. It may be because something didn't go your way or it may be for no reason in particular. The bottom line is you just feel stuck in a rut. Everyone has those types of days. I like to call them the "I wish I would've stayed in bed all day long" days. But the ironic thing about these days is that the last thing you want to do is hibernate under your covers.

As hard as it is to pull yourself out of bed, you have to. (That's an order.) Get in the shower, put on your favorite shoes, and get out there. (That's an order, too.) Go out with friends, go to the mall, go to the park, just go. Chances are you may still feel kind of crummy inside, but fake it on the outside. Laugh harder then usual, smile a lot, and pretend you are having fun. Push yourself to be social, especially in the times when it would be easier just to be alone. If you force yourself to get out there, there's a very good chance you won't have to pretend for very long at all.

LESSONS LEARNED THE HARD WAY:
1) REGARDLESS OF HOW YOU'RE FEELING, LIFE OUTSIDE YOUR BEDROOM WINDOW CONTINUES TO GO ON. 2) WHETHER YOU CHOOSE TO JOIN IT OR NOT IS COMPLETELY UP TO YOU. 3) TEN YEARS FROM NOW, LOOKING BACK, YOU WILL WISH YOU WOULD'VE JOINED IT.

stress busters

You've heard of ghost busters, but stress busters??? Stress busters are simple ways to awaken the great powers that exist inside each and every one of us, powers we sometimes forget we have when we need them the most, like confidence, and calmness, and super-duper strength. These qualities work together and can tackle any stress that comes your way.

Stress happens to all of us every single day. Every situation you encounter has the potential to be stressful depending on how you choose to deal with it. Making a peanut butter and jelly sandwich can be stressful if you worry about cutting yourself with the knife, but most likely, instead of worrying, you are thinking about how good the sandwich will taste when you eat it. That same control you have over yourself doing little things like making lunch is the same control you want to have over yourself when things become hectic and life gets overwhelming. Learning some stress-busting techniques is a sure-fire way to chase away the icky feelings stress brings on and use the remaining energy and adrenaline to work harder, reach higher, and bring you to success. Practice your stress busters, and let them help you to be strong, confident, and calm no matter what life brings.

LESSONS LEARNED THE HARD WAY: 1) EATING THREE CARTONS OF ICE CREAM IS NOT A GOOD WAY TO DEAL WITH STRESS. 2) NOT BEING ABLE TO FIT INTO YOUR PANTS CREATES MORE STRESS. 3) STRESSING ABOUT STRESS... WELL THAT'S JUST NEVER A GOOD THING.

stress-busting strategies

Breathe. You're thinking you breathe a zillion times a day and that hasn't ever helped you stress less. But deep breathing relaxes your entire body. Put your hand on your upper belly and take a long deep breath. Try to make your stomach expand, then exhale through your mouth releasing all the air you just took in. Repeat this three to five times and feel your body begin to relax.

Train your thoughts. Sometimes when you're stressed out your thoughts go wild and make you even more stressed. You think about what could happen instead of what is happening right now. In these times, try to concentrate on the moment and on taking it step by step. Instead of thinking "oh my goodness," think, "I can do this." Think positive thoughts. Think "I am smart," "I am beautiful," "I can get through this"... and you will.

Refuel. Often when life gets busy, we rush around trying to squish everything possible into our 24-hour days. We forget things, important things... like eating. No matter how stressed or busy you are, you should always make time to eat. Food gives you energy. It gives you brain power. It also gives you a quick break from whatever you are doing. Steer clear of sugary foods, like candy bars or cookies. These will give you a short spurt of energy and then make you sleepy. Fuel up on fruits, vegetables, and grains for a great boost.

Recharge. Get up and run around the block. Do some jumping jacks. Cartwheel across your kitchen. Find some kind of physical activity to wake up your muscles and get your blood moving. Stress causes your body to tense up; your muscles may cramp; your hands and feet may feel tingly. Get your body moving, and move closer to feeling your best.

Catch some zzz's. This one's simple. Make sure you sleep. No matter how much you have to do or how many thoughts are racing through your head, sacrificing sleep should never be an option. You need between eight to ten hours of sleep every night to feel well-rested, stress free, and ready to begin your day. Make sleep a priority, and your other priorities will fall into place.

feeling blue?

Regardless of how hard you try to keep your emotions in check, they can get the best of you. Yes, it is true that growing up is an emotional time. There is no doubt about that. But the emotional distress you encounter can be more than just mood swings. Sometimes it becomes more serious and you need more than just yourself to deal with it.

Depression can be very serious and dangerous if it continues over long periods of time. You may feel depressed because something in your life didn't work out as planned, but depression becomes a problem when you constantly find yourself feeling sad and even angry with yourself for no real reason.

If you feel that you may be depressed, it is very important to get help. Feeling depressed hurts, but it is something that can be fixed. Don't be afraid to talk about it with someone, such as a teacher, doctor, psychologist, or parent. If you don't feel comfortable talking to someone you know, jump online and check out the many websites that deal with depression. The first step is to determine if you are depressed and the second step is to talk to someone about it.

LESSONS LEARNED THE HARD WAY: 1) THE LONGER YOU WAIT TO GET HELP, THE LONGER IT TAKES TO GET BETTER. 2) TALKING TO A PROFESSIONAL DOES NOT MEAN YOU ARE CRAZY, WEAK, OR INSANE. IT JUST MEANS YOU NEED SOMEONE TO LISTEN TO YOU.

signs of depression

- feeling sad or hopeless

- loss of interest in most daily activities

- weight gain or weight loss

- sleeping too much or not enough

- lack of motivation

- grades in school may drop

- turning to drugs or alcohol

- feeling tired all the time

- feeling guilty for no real reason

- thinking often about death

- feeling anxious or worried

family

matters

AT ANY AGE, getting along with your FAMILY members is not always the easiest thing to do. You have PARENTS who, despite what they think, don't understand exactly how it is to be your age. You have SIBLINGS who compete in everything from getting GOOD GRADES in SCHOOL to getting your mother to love them more. And you have YOU, who sometimes has an urge to run as FAR AWAY as possible and other times wants to be the center of family ATTENTION.

Though it's sometimes EASIER just to shut your door, blast your music, and think about putting yourself up for adoption, try to REMEMBER that NO MATTER WHAT, family matters. They are the people who know you BEST and will always be the ones who love you most. So LEARNING the best way to deal with your family and with the situations you may encounter TOGETHER is not just an option, IT'S ESSENTIAL. Bottom line: No matter how crazy your family seems or how CRAZY they make you feel... family ALWAYS matters the most.

the parent trap

So let me guess… your parents treat you like a child. They set ridiculous rules and try to keep you from doing the fun stuff everybody else is doing. None of your friends' parents act that way, so why should yours? Here's the thing. Just as it is really hard being a kid these days, it's just as hard being a parent. (I know it's hard to believe, but it's the truth.) There's a lot of scary stuff that happens out there; your parents don't give you a curfew or forbid you to go to some party to make your life miserable. They do it because they love you and never want anything bad to happen to you.

So there's a few ways to deal with this. You can sneak out your window and risk a broken leg. You can lie to your parents and feel awful inside. Or you can be honest with them about how you feel, gain their trust, and live happily ever after. Okay, so maybe it's not that easy. But communicating with your parents will definitely make life a lot easier… for both of you. Give them details. Prove to them that they should trust you. Explain that if you ever find yourself in a situation that is over your head, you will call them. Creating a good relationship with your parents will save you a lot of heartache… and possibly a broken leg.

LESSONS LEARNED THE HARD WAY:
1) NO MATTER WHAT YOUR CURFEW IS, THERE'S ALWAYS SOMEONE OUT THERE WHO HAS TO BE HOME EARLIER. 2) RULES ARE LIKE LEGS — THEY AREN'T MADE TO BE BROKEN.

sibling rivalry

The first and most important thing you must remember is that no matter how much you look alike… think alike… act alike, you and your sibling are two very different people. You have your own likes and dislikes. Your own interests and hobbies. Your own strengths. Your own personalities. Your own successes and defeats.

People tend to compare siblings. People like parents, teachers, and friends. It can make you angry or resentful to feel that you have to live up to certain standards or expectations. Just because your sister or brother chooses one path doesn't mean you need to follow. It's up to you to find your own direction and to create your own goals to work toward achieving. When you succeed at something that you have chosen to do, not because of someone else, but because *you* choose it, you will feel incredible, and people will start to take notice. Don't compare yourself to your sibling or to anyone else for that matter. And always be the best "you" you can possibly be.

LESSONS LEARNED THE HARD WAY: 1) GROWING UP IN YOUR SIBLING'S SHADOW CAN MAKE YOU FEEL LIKE YOU'RE ALWAYS COMING IN SECOND PLACE. 2) THE ONLY WAY TO STEP OUT OF THAT SHADOW AND TAKE THE LEAD IS TO CREATE YOUR OWN PATH AND SHINE YOUR OWN LIGHT.

dealing with the big "d"

Divorce happens… a lot. It happens in all kinds of families to all kinds of kids. It is not something super unusual, and it is not something to feel ashamed of. No one wants to go through divorce, but sometimes it's the only way to make things okay again. When parents argue a lot it can make things unhappy and uncomfortable for everyone involved. Though divorce is sad because it causes separation, it can also bring happiness and relief because the fighting ends and everyone feels more at peace.

Parents decide to divorce for many different reasons, but none of those reasons is EVER because of their children. Doing poorly in school, not cleaning your room, breaking curfew, not eating your vegetables, and things like that DO NOT cause divorce. Nothing you do as a child could ever be the reason your parents decide to split up; that is one thing you can be absolutely sure of. The other thing you can be absolutely sure of is that even though parents separate, it does not mean they love their children any less. Divorce may cause a lot of changes, but no matter what happens, the love parents have for their children will never change.

LESSONS LEARNED THE HARD WAY: 1) CLEANING YOUR ROOM, TAKING OUT THE GARBAGE, COMING HOME EARLY, BEING ON YOUR BEST BEHAVIOR, SAYING PLEASE AND THANK YOU, AND BEING THE BEST CHILD IN THE WHOLE WORLD WILL NOT STOP YOUR PARENTS FROM GETTING A DIVORCE. 2) DOING THESE THINGS COULD POSSIBLY INCREASE YOUR ALLOWANCE AND MAYBE EVEN SCORE YOU THAT NEW BIKE YOU'VE BEEN WANTING.

breaking the mold

Since you were a little girl, you learned almost everything from your family… how to act, what to eat, how to interact with others, and what to believe in. As you grow older and go out in the world, you meet different people and experience different things. You expand your knowledge, outlook, and beliefs. As this happens you develop into a new person, picking and choosing the characteristics you want to be a part of you.

Many parents have a really hard time with this. You are their little girl and probably way before you were born they had this image in their head of exactly how you would be. As you develop, some of the things you come to value may be different from what your parents have instilled in you. Some of your dreams may lead you down a different path than they had hoped for you. That is okay. Learn as much as you can; expand your horizon. Be honest with yourself as to why you make the decisions you make and be honest with your family, as well. As long as your heart is in whatever you're doing, then what you are doing is meant to be. All that matters is your happiness, and when it comes down to it, that's what your parents care about the most.

LESSONS LEARNED THE HARD WAY:
1) RESEARCHING DIFFERENT RELIGIONS AND ATTENDING SERVICES AT DIFFERENT CHURCHES TO EXPAND YOUR HORIZONS AND LEARN NEW THINGS… GOOD IDEA. 2) DROPPING OUT OF SCHOOL, QUITTING YOUR JOB, DYEING YOUR HAIR FUCHSIA, AND HITCHHIKING ACROSS THE COUNTRY BECAUSE OF AN ARGUMENT YOU HAD WITH YOUR PARENTS… BAD IDEA.

You only get **ONE BODY**. It comes with **NO GUARANTEES**, no instructions, and no second chances, so the **CHOICES** you make **RIGHT NOW** are **EXTREMELY** important.

Your body needs **POSITIVE** thoughts, tender **CARE**, and **LOTS OF LOVE**. Your body needs **FOOD** and water, too. That's not too much to ask — **DON'T YOU AGREE?** Your **BODY** doesn't care what everyone else is doing; it is only **CONCERNED** with itself. That may sound a little bit **SELFISH**, and your body apologizes, but it wants to live the **LONGEST, HEALTHIEST** life possible. So, do **EVERYTHING** you can to ensure that **YOU** and your body will **ALWAYS** live happily **EVER AFTER**.

health conscious

Along with all the other changes going on in your body right now, your metabolism is changing also. This means that you aren't burning calories as fast as you used to. So in order to keep your changing body healthy, you need to change your eating and exercising habits as well. (Insert BIG *grunt* here.)

Being healthy can seem like a huge pain sometimes, but it's really easy once you get started. The point is not to eliminate things like sugars, fats, and carbohydrates from your diet, but to try to limit them, and eat lots of protein. If you want to lose a few pounds, you don't need to go on a diet; you need to start eating healthier. Oh, and don't forget about exercise. (Insert another BIG *grunt* here.) You don't need to run on a treadmill for hours to burn calories. You can walk, run, bike, dance, swim, or do any other physical activity that gets your heartbeat up and the sweat dripping.

When you combine eating healthily and exercising three to four times a week, you will not only see a difference when you look in the mirror, but you will also see a change in your attitude and in the amount of energy you have. When your body is happy and healthy, your entire self reaps the benefits.

LESSONS LEARNED THE HARD WAY: 1) EATING GRAPEFRUIT FOR BREAKFAST, LUNCH, AND DINNER IS BY NO MEANS HEALTHY, AND THE WEIGHT YOU DROP WILL INEVITABLY FIND ITS WAY BACK.
2) RAISING THE SPOON FROM YOUR PLATE TO YOUR MOUTH DOES NOT CONSTITUTE EXERCISE.

body pollution

There is a certain curiosity that comes with growing up, a certain desire for experimentation. The thing is, before putting anything foreign into your body, such as drugs, alcohol, or cigarette smoke, you should learn as much as you can about them and about the effects they can have on your body. Knowing that everyone else is doing it isn't enough. Each person's body reacts differently to certain substances. There's no way of telling how your body will react to drugs, alcohol, or cigarettes. Just trying something once can affect you more than you might think. You are the only person who can decide if it's worth taking that risk.

The risks that come with using drugs or alcohol span further than just the physical effects. Once you are under their influence, there's no telling what can happen, and it is very easy to find yourself in a situation that you may not be able to handle. You can't plan to stay in control. That's the scariest part. Once you choose to let a foreign substance into your body, that substance is free to take over. Before you give something that much power, make sure you are ready to deal with the risks involved, both short-term and long-term.

LESSONS LEARNED THE HARD WAY: 1) TOBACCO KILLS OVER A MILLION PEOPLE EACH YEAR. 2) DRUGS AND/OR ALCOHOL PLAY A ROLE IN MANY RAPES AND SEXUAL ASSAULTS. 3) KIDS WHO USE "GATEWAY DRUGS," SUCH AS TOBACCO OR ALCOHOL, ARE MUCH MORE LIKELY TO USE COCAINE AND OTHER HARD DRUGS.

what's eating you?

There's no cute little introduction or smooth way of talking around this topic to avoid freaking you out. In fact, I want to freak you out. I want you to know that **eating disorders can kill you**. That's the bottom line. When how much you weigh and what you eat becomes your life... when you become obsessed with stepping on the scale or with staring at your body in the mirror, you have a problem and you need to deal with it before it is too late.

Many girls think they are in complete control of their eating habits. They diet but don't think they have an eating disorder because to them an eating disorder is a sickness. They don't see themselves as being sick. The scary thing is, most eating disorders start out as simple diets, but they eventually get out of control.

Looking good is a huge pressure on girls growing up, so it is easy to become obsessed with things like how much you weigh or what size pants you fit into. Stepping over the edge into an eating disorder is extremely easy to do and is, sadly, so common among young girls. Knowing the signs and understanding the severity of these disorders can help to save a life.

LESSONS LEARNED THE HARD WAY: 1) YOU NEED FOOD TO LIVE. 2) ONE PIECE OF LETTUCE OR A FEW CORN FLAKES DOES NOT CONSTITUTE A MEAL. 3) IF YOU THINK THEY DO, GET HELP.

three common eating disorders

anorexia nervosa: A refusal to eat, leading to self-starvation. Usually the person is very thin but has a distorted view that she is fat.

bulimia nervosa: Eating too much food and feeling out of control when doing so, then getting rid of the food by vomiting or using laxatives and /or diuretics.

compulsive overeating disorder: Eating excessively, leading to obesity. Usually the person goes on crash diets, but shortly after losing weight, goes back to food binging.

a person with an eating disorder may...

- fixate on food, calories, eating, dieting, weight, and body shape,
- feel fat no matter how much weight is lost,
- diet or exercise excessively,
- eat alone, or hide eating and food, or hide weight gain or loss,
- eat large amounts of food in a short time,
- purge after eating,
- strive to do things perfectly and be perfect,
- withdraw from friends or family,
- feel guilty after eating,
- feel afraid of gaining weight,
- hoard food, and/or
- spend a lot of time in the bathroom after eating.

— Gladys Folkers, MA,
and Jeanne Engelmann

saving face

You could swear your pimples have brains of their own, their own pulses and heartbeats, as well as their own motives for planting themselves on your face at the worst possible times ever. Pimples are unfortunately a part of life. And since they don't give much notice before dropping by for a visit, you want to know how to handle them when they arrive and how to do your best to keep them from coming back.

No, it's not true that eating a chocolate bar or a bag of potato chips will plague you with acne for the rest of your life, but that is by no means an invitation for you to run out and eat unhealthy foods as much as you want to. What you put into your body will eventually come out, not only in the way you are thinking, but also through the pores in your skin. So, steering clear of greasy, fatty, and oily foods and drinking lots of water are good ways to limit the number of breakouts you will have. Another way to keep your pores unclogged and your skin healthy is to be sure to wash your face and body after exercising or doing anything that makes you sweat a lot.

When pimples do arise, don't do all the things you want to do, i.e., scrub, rub, pick, poke, zap, etc. Yes, it is important to keep your skin clean, but applying layers of medication will dry out your skin and may even cause more outbreaks. Keep it simple. If that doesn't work and you are feeling as if pimples are ruining your life, you may want to make an appointment with the dermatologist (a pimple genius) or even talk with your regular doctor about prescribing a special medication.

LESSONS LEARNED THE HARD WAY: 1) PIMPLES CANNOT BE BURNED OFF YOUR FACE WITH A CURLING IRON. 2) TAPING AN ASTRINGENT PAD TO YOUR FACE WILL LEAVE A HUGE RED MARK AND WON'T MAKE THE PIMPLE GO AWAY ANY FASTER.

what? how? when? where? why?

You only get one body so you have the right to ask as many questions as you need to in order to know as much about it as possible. If something feels wrong, you should want to know how to make it right. If you're thinking about trying something new, you should want to know how your body would be affected by it.

Sure, it may be hard for you to get certain words out of your mouth without cracking a smile or feeling all funny inside, but just because you feel uncomfortable about certain topics doesn't mean they are wrong to ask about. Doctors, pharmacists, counselors — even your parents — will not be fazed by your questions. They have heard much, much worse, and are capable of handling pretty much anything. Make sure you have a doctor that you feel comfortable talking with, and if you don't, ask around and try to find a new one who will make you feel at ease regardless of the topic of your conversation.

Do your best to know as much about your body as possible and about the way it works... and if there is ever a doubt or question in your mind about either of those things, ask, research, call, surf the Web... do whatever it takes to get yourself informed.

LESSONS LEARNED THE HARD WAY: 1) THE DOCTOR HAS TREATED RASHES IN UNGODLY PLACES AND STUCK HIS OR HER FINGERS IN PLACES THEY PROBABLY SHOULDN'T BE STUCK. 2) FOR HIM OR HER, TALKING ABOUT THINGS SUCH AS DIARRHEA, MENSTRUATION, AND FLATULENCE IS LIKE TALKING ABOUT THE WEATHER. 3) IF ANY PART OF YOUR BODY FEELS DIFFERENT THAN USUAL, YOU SHOULD MOST LIKELY GET IT CHECKED OUT.

checking in below the belt

The thought of visiting a gynecologist and having someone you don't know very well snooping around in your most private of private areas isn't something anyone really enjoys. But it's just one of those wonderful things that comes with being a girl (as if PMS and menstrual cramps aren't enough).

Though it may not be the most pleasant of experiences, visiting a gynecologist is a huge part of being healthy. Most experts agree that if you are sexually active, thinking of becoming sexually active, or are over 18 years old, you should visit a gynecologist once a year. If before that time anything feels unusual down there, make an appointment. This is one body part you don't want to take any chances with.

The visit really isn't *that* bad. You and your doctor will first discuss your medical history as well as any other concerns you have. This is your chance to talk about birth control, sexually transmitted diseases, or anything else on your mind. And don't worry, whatever you discuss with your doctor will stay between you and your doctor. The exam will consist of a breast exam (painless) followed by an internal exam (a bit uncomfortable but not painful). The doctor will check around inside your vagina to make sure all is well, quickly do a Pap smear (touch your cervix with a long skinny swab) to check for cervical cancer, and then send you on your way. The best news: you don't have to go back for another whole year.

LESSONS LEARNED THE HARD WAY: 1) THE GYNECOLOGIST HAS SEEN A MILLION VAGINAS BEFORE YOURS, SO THE CHANCES OF YOURS BEING ANY DIFFERENT IS PROBABLY ABOUT SLIM TO NONE. 2) WHEN YOU REACH THIS AGE, STIRRUPS ARE NO LONGER JUST FOR HORSES.

to do it or not to do it

It doesn't matter if everyone's doing it or if no one is doing it at all. What matters is how you feel inside, how you'll feel tomorrow, and how you'll feel five years down the line looking back. It's not about your boyfriend or your parents or your best friend; it's about you — your mind, your heart, and your body.

Having sex is not just about the moment; it's about the million things that come after. Think about all the risks involved before the moment even arrives... and yes, there are many. There are the endless number of sexually transmitted diseases that once you get *do not* go away... there is the chance that you could become pregnant, and that alone begins a whole new list that you may or may not be ready to deal with. There is the chance that you may have regrets shortly after and will be unable to take it back. There is the possibility that while you are thinking more about the emotional part, he is thinking more about the physical. Trust me, the list goes on.

A huge part of being healthy and loving yourself is having the greatest respect possible for your body. Check in with yourself and make your own personal decisions about what you are and aren't ready for. Yes, it is true that you are growing up, and you are making your own decisions and having new experiences. Just remember, though, that in that growth you don't only have the freedom to have sex — you also have the freedom to say no.

LESSONS LEARNED THE HARD WAY: 1) THE TWO MINUTES SPENT WAITING FOR THE RESULTS OF THE PREGNANCY TEST AREN'T WORTH ANY OF THE MINUTES SPENT IN HIS BED. 2) HIS SAYING YOU ARE HIS FIRST DOESN'T NECESSARILY MEAN YOU ARE HIS FIRST. 3) WHEN YOU REALLY FALL IN LOVE, YOU MIGHT WISH YOU COULD TAKE BACK ALL THE OTHERS. 4) YOU CAN'T TAKE IT BACK.

the
truth
about
the plastic
princess

You **GREW UP** playing with **BARBIE**, with her perfect **PINK DRESSES** and incredibly astounding posture, her **AWESOME** golden locks, **TEENY TINY** waistline, and perfectly **PERKY BREASTS**. You probably wanted to be just like her when you **GREW UP**.

Now you're **OLD ENOUGH** to know the **TRUTH**. Barbie is an unachievable **IDEAL**. Thanks to the **BRILLIANCE** of computer **TECHNOLOGY** and numerous **ROLLS** of duct tape, this Barbie-look becomes **ACHIEVABLE** to the girls on many magazine covers. **STRIVING** to be like them is **WASTE** of your time, and **STARVING** yourself to look like them is a waste of **YOUR LIFE**. Be **PROUD** of who you are, and **BE THE BEST** you can possibly be. And anytime you look in the **MIRROR** and feel a little down, remember this: If **BARBIE** had a **HEARTBEAT** and roamed the earth, chances are she'd ask for a big fat **ICE-CREAM SUNDAE** with **LOTS** of **WHIPPED CREAM** on top, right before falling over because of her **TINY BODY'S** inability to hold up her **ENORMOUS** breasts.

cover girl

Those girls on the cover of the most recent fashion magazines may look incredibly perfect, but looks can be very deceiving. It's all in the magic of editing, airbrushing, cutting-and-pasting, push-up bras, tummy tuckers, and whatever other concoctions they use to make us think the "perfect person" actually exists.

We are bombarded with images of supermodels and starlets; we are brought up thinking that they are what defines beauty. Personally, I think this world would be a much better place if instead of telling us the brand name of the model's dress or the shade of her lipstick, we were informed of what she really ate for breakfast or of how many rolls of duct tape were used to get her breasts to stand up that high.

Unfortunately, the world doesn't work that way, so we need to remember to insert our own side-notes when looking at magazines, movies, and television in order to put it all into some kind of perspective (as well as to maintain our own personal sanity and give us a couple of laughs). Keep all this in mind the next time you see a "perfect body" and wish it was yours. Chances are it isn't so perfect, or that the owner of it is a very hungry lady.

LESSONS LEARNED THE HARD WAY: 1) DUCT TAPING YOUR BREASTS CLOSER TOGETHER FOR ADDITIONAL CLEAVAGE MAY SEEM LIKE A GOOD IDEA AT THE TIME. 2) REMOVING THE DUCT TAPE LATER THAT DAY...OOOOUUUUCH!

filling up the cup

Breasts: why this one part of the female anatomy creates such chaos, the world will never know. But we do know this: developing breasts can be a very overwhelming process. We can't stop our breasts from growing, and we can't force them to grow if they're not ready to (despite what the latest miracle drug promises). It takes about five years for breasts to develop fully, and that's just on average. Some girls don't fully develop until they turn twenty-something, and other girls are finished growing by the time they are fifteen. So take a deep breath, and prepare yourself for anything.

Standing in the mirror staring at them won't make your breasts go away, and doing countless exercises humming the "I Must Increase My Bust" song... well, that won't do anything either. Your body is going through incredible changes, and though it can be extremely overwhelming at times, you are not going through it alone. The cover-up, push-up, padding, stuffing, minimizing process is all around you; you are definitely one among a million who have gone through this before, as well as one among a million who are going through it now. So stop your worrying — the likelihood that your breasts (or lack thereof) are going to make news headlines is slim to none.

LESSONS LEARNED THE HARD WAY: 1) IF YOU STUFF YOUR BRA WITH TISSUES THERE IS NO GUARANTEE THAT THEY WILL STAY EXACTLY WHERE YOU PUT THEM. 2) THE TISSUES MAY HAPPEN TO MAKE THEIR WAY UP OUT OF YOUR BRA AND TO THE TOP OF YOUR DRESS. 3) IF A BOY YOU HAVE A CRUSH ON POINTS OUT TO YOU THAT THIS HAS HAPPENED, YOU WILL IMMEDIATELY TURN RED AND MAY LATER ACQUIRE SOME UNWANTED NICKNAMES.

being the best you

The chances of waking up one morning with a brand-new body or a brand-new life are probably slim. It is a complete waste of time to sit around sulking because your legs are too short or your nose is too big or your breasts are too small or whatever it is about you that makes you unhappy. There are things you can change and there are things that you can't. Learning to deal with the things you can't change and making the effort to change the things you can is a huge part of loving yourself.

Check in with yourself and figure out what you can do to be the best "you" possible. If it means eating healthier and working out so that you can stop hating your thighs or your tummy or whatever body part it is that drives you crazy, then do it. If you spend your evenings being lazy and feeling down, find an activity or join a sports team; do anything that will improve the time you spend on your own. If you stare at yourself in the mirror and aren't happy with what you see, go get a haircut or treat yourself to a makeover to bring out the best in your appearance. Your life is yours to revamp and change at any time you need to. Do whatever it takes to be the best you that you can be.

LESSONS LEARNED THE HARD WAY: 1) THE BEST 'YOU' IS DEFINITELY NOT BROUGHT OUT BY LOCKING YOURSELF IN YOUR ROOM BECAUSE YOU THINK YOU LOOK FAT IN YOUR PROM DRESS. 2) YOU WILL FEEL SAD WHEN YOU LOOK AT YOUR FRIENDS' PROM PICTURES AND YOU ARE NOT IN THEM.

boy poll

Throughout the years, I have polled many males to see what it is they really look for in a girl. I assumed I'd find out two things. One: that the big-breasted, tiny-waisted Barbie-doll girl was what they wanted, and two: my body and I were definitely out of luck. Lucky for me and for the zillion other girls who don't resemble the doll we played with as children, my assumptions were completely wrong.

It has been stated time and time again that although cover girls, Barbie-type women are nice to look at, they are by no means the kind of girls most men want to date. Boys like a *real* girl... a girl who eats a huge dinner consisting of more than a few pieces of lettuce... a girl they can hug without being afraid she will break in half if squeezed too hard... a girl who has more to offer than just a pretty face. A guy wants to date a girl he can be himself around, a girl he knows is being herself around him. So there's no need to fret that your minor imperfections may leave you boyfriendless and alone. In the boy poll, being yourself and being real rates you in the top ten.

LESSONS LEARNED THE HARD WAY: 1) BOYS ARE NOT BLIND OR DUMB. 2) THEY KNOW ALL ABOUT THE MAGIC OF PADDED BRAS, CONTROL-TOP PANTYHOSE, TWO POUNDS OF MAKEUP, PLATFORM SHOES, AND FAKE FINGERNAILS. 3) THEY ALSO KNOW WHAT KIND OF GIRL THEY WOULD WANT TO BRING HOME TO MOM.

LOVING YOURSELF is the **BEST WAY** to live your life. **LET'S FACE IT**... it's the **ONLY** way to live your life (well... **HAPPILY**, that is). Loving yourself all comes **DOWN TO YOU**. And it's not a **SIMPLE** thing to do. It takes **LOTS** of **CONFIDENCE** and **LITTLE** self-criticism. Loving yourself comes from the **COMFORT** of just being the **REAL YOU** and from surrounding yourself with people who know you best and **LOVE YOU** for being you.

Growing up and **FITTING IN** and feeling good are **FAR FROM EASY**, but if you believe in yourself and head toward **YOUR DREAMS** (and **HUG YOURSELF** every once in a while), everything else will **SOMEHOW** fall into place. When things get **BAD** (and they probably will) **CHECK IN** with yourself and see if **MAYBE** you could use some extra **HELP**. You can't do **EVERYTHING** single-handedly **ALL** the time.

Love yourself — **EACH AND EVERY** single part — from your **LITTLE** pinky toe to your great **BIG** mind and all those other **PARTS** in between. Make the decision to **LOVE YOURSELF**. You **DESERVE** nothing less.

how to love yourself
a little bit more

1. Make a list of your very best qualities and hang it on your mirror to look at when you get ready each morning.

2. Pick yourself some dandelions on your walk home from school and put them in a vase on your nightstand to brighten up your bedroom.

3. Rent your favorite movie and have a few of your closest friends over to watch it with you.

4. Eat a banana or apple with your lunch instead of a plate of greasy French fries.

5. Write yourself a love poem.

6. Create a scrapbook with pictures of your family. Anytime you feel upset or angry with any of your family members, look at the book and remind yourself of all the good times you've had together.

7. On Monday make a list of everything you need to do by Friday. On Friday if everything is checked off on your list take a trip to the mall and treat yourself to something special.

8. If you are feeling sad, read a joke book until you can't stop laughing.

9. When your mirror is steamed up after your shower, write "I Love You" on it with your finger. The next time you shower again it will make you smile.

10. Have your mom or dad buy fresh vegetables when they go grocery shopping. The next time you watch TV you can "veg out" for real.

11. Give yourself a BIG hug every day.

12. Find an old picture of yourself from when you were a little girl. Hang it in your locker as a reminder of how carefree and happy you can be.

13. Have a sleepover party with your favorite friends. Have everyone bring mud masks, nail polish, hair accessories, and anything else perfect for an evening of beauty.

14. Instead of reading a fashion magazine, read a magazine about something you know nothing about.

15. Make really silly faces at yourself in the mirror.

16. Do something nice for someone. Give them a batch of homemade cookies or share your lunch with someone who forgot theirs. It'll make you feel good about yourself, and make someone else feel good, too.

17. Talk to someone new at school today. Who knows — you could end up making a friend.

18. Instead of buying the same black shirt everyone else is wearing, buy a different shirt in bright red and make a fashion statement.

19. Make up a positive affirmation like "I love myself" or "I can do anything." Repeat it to yourself whenever you're feeling scared, insecure, or down on yourself.

20. Create your own website. Include your favorite pictures of yourself and the people who matter most to you, along with a list of hobbies, dreams, and other cool stuff you've done. Think of it as your own personal brag spot in cyberspace.

if you need a little help:
WEBSITES

www.selfesteem.org
This site provides information about the importance of self-esteem, how to build it, and why you need it in your life. It provides inspirational stories as well as uplifting words to help you raise your self-esteem and live a happy life.

www.bodypositive.com
BodyPositive looks at ways to feel good in the body you have, and reminds you that your body hears everything you think.

www.kidshealth.org
KidsHealth is the largest and most visited site on the Web providing doctor-approved health information about children from before birth through adolescence. It has information on every subject you can possibly imagine dealing with emotional, mental, and physical health.

www.depressedteens.com
An educational site dedicated to helping teenagers and their parents and educators understand the signs and symptoms of teenage depression. It provides resources for those ready to reach out and get the help they need.

www.teengrowth.com
TeenGrowth is a website thousands of teens continue to turn to for health information. Board-certified physicians give the scoop on puberty, family, friends, drugs, sex, and emotions.

www.gottaquit.com
This site gives accurate information about the physical and social effects of smoking as well as tips on how to quit the habit.